PHILADELPHIA
COLORING BOOK & HISTORY
By Anna Nadler

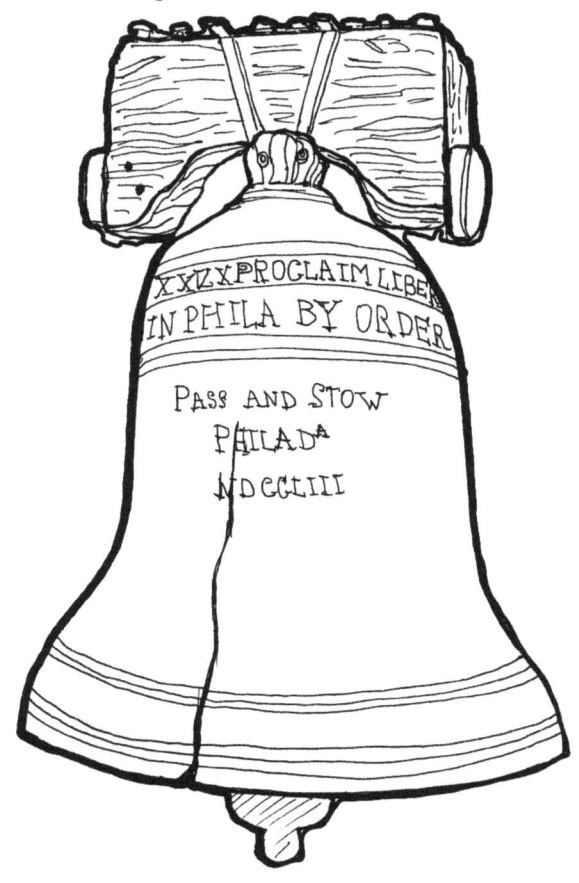

ISBN: 9781958428344

City Hall

When you visit Philadelphia, no doubt you will be simply in awe of Philadelphia City Hall, as soon as you see it. The City Hall is a grand structure that took 30 years and 25 million dollars to build. Its construction started in 1872 and it was completed in 1901. The building is 548 feet by 470 feet and it is seven stories high.

The building was designed by architects John McArthur Jr. and Thomas Ustick Walter, in the architectural style called Second Empire. At the time, it was designed to be the world's tallest building, surpassing its contemporaries - the Washington Monument and the Eiffel Tower. The building's materials include granite and brick.

Stonemason William Struthers and sculptor Alexander Milne Calder had designed more than 250 sculptures adorning the structure. These sculptures depict artists, engineers, and teachers of the time, who played an important part in the development of the city.

While City Hall's tower was completed by 1894, the interior was not finished until 1901. The building is located in the center of Penn Square.

Philadelphia Museum of Art
& the Rocky Statue

Located at 2600 Benjamin Franklin Parkway, the
Philadelphia Museum of Art is one of America's
oldest museums, with one of the finest collections.
The museum was established in 1876 and the
construction of the museum's main building
was completed in 1928.

Its curated collection features over 240,000 objects
of European, Asian and American origin.
They range from sculptures, installations, paintings,
to prints, armor, photography and decorative art.

The 72 stone steps leading up to the entrance of the
museum are known as "Rocky Steps", made famous by
the 1976 film - Rocky. Many people like to mimic
running up these steps, like Rocky did in the movie.
Once you climb on top of the stairs, you will get a
fantastic view of Eakins Oval and Philadelphia City Hall.

The Rocky statue, featuring his famous pose, is located
at the bottom right of the steps. It makes for a great
photo opportunity when you visit the museum.

Rodin Museum

Located at 2151 Benjamin Franklin Parkway, this Beaux-Arts style building and garden holds one of the largest collections of sculptor Auguste Rodin's work, outside of France; 150 objects in all, made of bronze, marble, and plaster.

The museum was a gift of a movie-theatre magnate, Jules Mastbaum to the city of Philadelphia, in 1929.

Some of the famous Rodin works included in the collection are "The Thinker," "The Kiss," "Eternal Springtime," and many more.

The garden has sculptures of "The Three Shades" and "The Burghers of Calais." Also featured are elaborate "Gates of Hell" doors that captivate the imagination, a project that took Rodin 37 years to create and modify.

Rodin Museum is considered part of Philadelphia Museum of Art. It is located nearby.

Swann Memorial Fountain

The design of the Swann Memorial Fountain,
or Fountain of the Three Rivers was created by
artist Alexander Calder and architect Wilson Eyre
in 1924. The fountain honors Wilson Cary Swann,
founder of the Philadelphia Fountain Society.

The symbolism of the sculptures is in the tradition
of "river god" sculpture. Depicted are large Native
American figures to represent the area's major streams,
the Delaware, the Schuylkill, and the Wissahickon.
The frogs and turtles pour water toward the
50-foot geyser in the center. Swans are a play on
Dr. Swann's name.

The fountain is located in the area of Logan Circle,
or Logan Square, near Benjamin Franklin Parkway.
It is surrounded by beautiful landscaping, flowers,
and has a backdrop of beautiful historical buildings.
Visitors can sit on the many benches around the
circle and enjoy the glorious views as well as
the refreshing water drops from the fountain.

LIBERTY BELL

Probably the most famous symbol of Philadelphia, and American Independence, the Liberty Bell is also known as Old State House Bell.

It was made in 1752 by Whitechapel Bell Foundry, is about 4 feet tall, and weighs 2,080 pounds.

The inscription on the bell reads:

Proclaim LIBERTY Throughout all the Land unto all the Inhabitants Thereof Lev. XXV. v X.
By Order of the ASSEMBLY of the Province of PENSYLVANIA for the State House in PhiladA
Pass and Stow
Philada
MDCCLIII

It was originally located in the steeple of the State House, now known as Independence Hall. Currently the bell occupies the Liberty Bell Center, in Independence National Historical Park.

The bell got its iconic crack in the early 19th century. Some claim that it cracked while ringing for the death of Chief Justice John Marshall in 1835.

Eastern State Penitentiary

Eastern State Penitentiary is located at 2027 Fairmount Avenue, in Philadelphia. It was operational 1829 - 1971. The prison was originally named Cherry Hill State Prison due to its location on Cherry Hill farmland. It was designed by John Haviland and opened on October 25, 1829.

Eastern State's came up with a revolutionary system of incarceration, dubbed the "Pennsylvania system" or separate system. Its main feature was separate confinement as a form of rehabilitation. The warden had to visit every inmate every single day. It was considered to be the world's first true penitentiary, and had less than 400 prisoners during its years of operation.

In 1994, Eastern State opened to the public for history tours. Today it is a museum and historic site, open for visitors and events year-round. You can take a guided tour or a self-guided audio tour narrated by Steve Buscemi. There is also a scavenger hunt for children. You can view their photo gallery and walk into several specially marked solitary confinement cells, some of which have movies playing inside. Most cells are off limits and filled with years' worth of rubble and debris.

THE MÜTTER MUSEUM

Considered to be America's finest museum of medical history, the Mütter Museum began as a donation from American surgeon Thomas Dent Mütter, MD (1811-1859) In 1863 the first building for the museum was completed, located on Locust and 13th Streets. Since 1909 the museum has moved to 19 South 22nd Street. Since Dr. Mütter's donation of 1,700 objects, the Museum collection has expanded to include more than 25,000 objects.

The Museum has garnered international popularity and has been featured in a film, Discovery Channel documentary, and two bestselling books.
When you visit, you will find well preserved collections of anatomical specimens, models, and medical instruments, video demonstrations of operations, medical curiosities and abnormalities, and more.

The Mütter Museum shines a light on many mysteries of the human body. It also teaches us to appreciate the history and advancements of diagnosis and treatment of various diseases. The museum sees over 130,000 visitors annually.

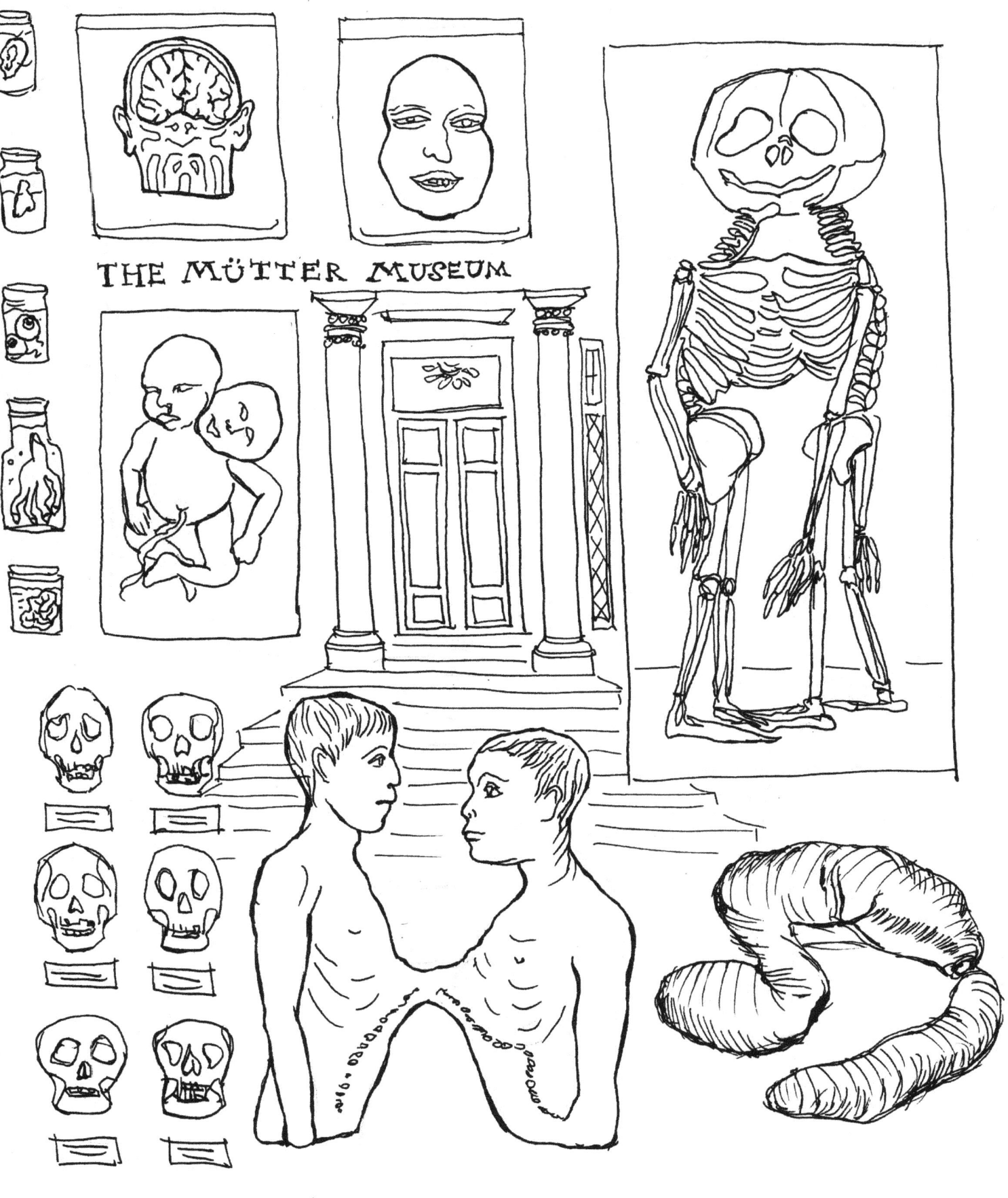

THE MÜTTER MUSEUM

PHILLY CHEESESTEAK

Perhaps no other food is as synonymous with the city of Philadelphia as the famous Philly Cheesesteak.

It traditionally is made up of thinly-sliced chopped ribeye steak topped with melted American cheese, provolone cheese, or Cheez Whiz. Served on a hoagie roll with toppings like fried onions, or fried bell peppers.

The cheesesteak came about in the early 20th century. According to a 1987 exhibition catalog published by the Library Company of Philadelphia and the Historical Society of Pennsylvania - "by combining frizzled beef, onions, and cheese in a small loaf of bread."

Pat and Harry Olivieri are said to have invented the sandwich by serving chopped steak on an Italian roll in the early 1930s. Later becoming known as "Pat's King of Steaks."

Today there are many restaurants in Philadelphia serving this delicious and affordable fast food.

Franklin Institute

The Franklin Institute is a gorgeous and majestic building that houses a science museum in Philadelphia. It is located at 222 North 20th Street.

It was originally established in 1824, by Samuel Vaughan Merrick and William H. Keating, as The Franklin Institute of the State of Pennsylvania for the Promotion of the Mechanic Arts. The Institute offered classes in mechanics, drafting, and engineering. It promoted science and invention.

Despite the Great Depression of the 1930s, the Franklin Institute and the Poor Richard Club started to build a new science museum and memorial hall. The community quickly contributed $5.1 million, and in 1932, the cornerstone of the new Franklin Institute was laid at 20th Street and the Benjamin Franklin Parkway.

Today, the Institute continues its educational legacy. As stated on their web page: "In the spirit of inquiry and discovery embodied by Benjamin Franklin, the mission of The Franklin Institute is to inspire a passion for learning about science and technology."

RITTENHOUSE SQUARE PARK

Rittenhouse Square Park is one of the five original open-space parks planned by William Penn and his surveyor Thomas Holme in 1682. It is the fourth oldest park in the United States. Rittenhouse Square neighborhood is one of the most expensive and luxurious areas in Philadelphia.

Named for astronomer and clockmaker David Rittenhouse, the park is a welcoming spot for painters, families, and all people looking for peace and relaxation in the city.

Rittenhouse Square Park is taken care of by the non-profit group called The Friends of Rittenhouse Square. The park is located at 1800 Walnut St, Philadelphia and spans about two short blocks on all sides.

You can view the iconic park kiosk, as well as many sculptures like "Lion Crushing a Serpent" as well as "Duck Girl" and "Billy," a two-foot-high bronze billy goat.

High-rise residences with luxury apartments overlook the beautiful park. There are also fine dining restaurants, luxury retail stores and more.

BARNES FOUNDATION

The Barnes Foundation is an art collection and educational institution that promotes the love of art and horticulture. It is located at 2025 Benjamin Franklin Parkway in Philadelphia. The foundation owns more than 4,000 objects, including over 900 paintings, with an estimated value at $25 billion.

Albert C. Barnes (1872–1951), a Philaldelphia art collector, chartered the Barnes in 1922. His goal was to teach people from all backgrounds and walks of life how to look at and appreciate art.

It took Dr. Barnes thirty years to collect masterpiece paintings of impressionist, post-impressionist, and modern eras, including Cézanne, Renoir, Matisse, Picasso and Modigliani. Also displayed are African masks, native American jewelry, Greek antiquities, and decorative metalwork.

When you visit you will note Cubist bas-reliefs on the main building, by sculptor Jacques Lipchitz. African art decorates the outside wrought iron, with tile work by the Enfield Pottery and Tile Works on the front portico of the building.

UNIVERSITY OF PENNSYLVANIA

A private Ivy League research university,
University of Pennsylvania was founded in 1740.
The university has four undergraduate schools
and 12 graduate and professional schools.

Benjamin Franklin was one of the university's founders.
He advocated for an educational institution that trained
leaders in academia, commerce, and public service.

It fits the textbook definition of an Ivy League school.
It has beautiful Gothic architecture and lush courtyards.
On grounds you will also discover art by Alexander
Calder, "Brick House," a new Simone Leigh sculpture,
and a statue of Ben Franklin on a bench. There is also
Franklin Field, the country's oldest operating football
stadium - a home of the Penn Relays.

MONUMENT TO SIX MILLION JEWISH MARTYRS

Monument to Six Million Jewish Martyrs, is part of Horwitz-Wasserman Holocaust Memorial Plaza, located at 16th Street and the Benjamin Franklin Parkway. This plaza is dedicated to honoring the memory of the Jewish people who perished in the Holocaust, as well as educating people about the unspeakable atrocities that happened during that time and what lead up to them.

Monument to Six Million Jewish Martyrs was created by sculptor Nathan Rapoport in 1964. It is 18 feet tall, weighs 5 tons, and is made of bronze, cast in Pietrasanta, Italy. The subjects depicted in the sculpture symbolize a blend of suffering and heroism. Women, men and children are enveloped by flames, reaching vertically. The emotions are sometimes of despair, prayer, fighting and hope.

The sculpture rests on a granite base, inscribed on four sides. One of the inscriptions reads: "In memory of the six million Jewish Holy Souls, who persevered through the Nazis 1933-1945. Remember our brothers, the Holiness of HaShem, who were murdered at the hands of the Nazis."

THE HOLOCAUST

ACADEMY OF MUSIC

Academy of Music is located at 240 S. Broad Street in Philadelphia, in the Avenue of the Arts area.
Known as "The Grand Old Lady of Locust Street," the hall is the oldest opera house in the US, built in 1857 by Napoleon LeBrun who modeled its lavish interior after La Scala Opera House in Milan.

It is considered Philadelphia's most revered performing space. It has a brick and gaslit facade, with a grand interior of scarlet with gold caryatids and a 5,000-pound crystal chandelier.

Academy of Music was home to the Philadelphia Orchestra 1900 - 2001, who maintains ownership of the Academy. It returns every January to play the Academy Anniversary Concert and Ball.

Academy of Music was designated a National Historic Landmark in 1962.

Carpenters' Hall

Carpenters' Hall, located at 320 Chestnut Street
in Philadelphia, was built in 1770–1774.
The architect who designed it, Robert Smith,
created it in Georgian architectural style.

Carpenters' Hall is known as the birthplace of
the Commonwealth of Pennsylvania. It is
part of Independence National Historical Park.

The building was built for the Carpenters' Company of
the City and County of Philadelphia - the country's
oldest extant craft guild. It was completed in 1775,
as a two-story brick meeting hall.

The First Continental Congress, held there in 1774,
was the first time that Americans of different
political affiliations met to debate various issues.

INDEPENDENCE HALL

Independence Hall is located at 520 Chestnut Street between 5th and 6th Streets.

It is a landmark historical building, designated in 1979. In the 1700s, America's Founding Fathers debated and adopted the United States Declaration of Independence and the Constitution.

It is located at the center of Independence National Historical Park. Independence Hall was added to the National Register of Historic Places in 1966 and as a World Heritage Site in 1979.

The building was known as Pennsylvania State House, when it was completed in 1753. It was the capitol of both the United States and of the Province and later the Commonwealth of Pennsylvania.
Second Continental Congress was held there from 1775 to 1781. It was also the site of the Constitutional Convention in 1788.

In 1973, a replica of the Thomas Stretch clock was restored to Independence Hall.

THE BETSY ROSS HOUSE

The Betsy Ross House is located at 239 Arch Street in Philadelphia's historic district. Betsy Ross or Elizabeth Griscom, (1752–1836) was a renowned seamstress and flag maker in 1700s, famous for making the first American flag. She lived and worked running her business from her house in the 18th century.

She was a widow with seven children, having been married three times, but losing her husbands in the war. She managed to run a prosperous business with her sewing skills.

When she was 24, Betsy started an upholstery business with her husband, John Ross, sewing flags, uniforms, tents, bedding and other items. Unfortunately he passed away, and a few years after, Ross remarried. She continued to run her business, sewing for the Continental Army. The second husband died as well. Finally, in 1883, Betsy married her third husband, John Claypoole, with whom she lived for 34 years. Ross continued to work until she retired at 76 years old.

To celebrate the 200-year anniversary of her birth, the Betsy Ross stamp was issued in 1952. On it was an image of Betsy Ross with the flag on her lap.

Philadelphia's Magic Gardens

Philadelphia's Magic Gardens is a magical, sparkly wonderland that immerses you in a variety of mixed media art entirely made of mosaics. Its original creator, Isaiah Zagar, used multi color bottles, handmade tiles, bicycle wheels, mirrors, as well as primitive folk art in his work. You can marvel at the walls and steps for many hours and discover more and more surprising details.

Philadelphia's Magic Gardens now operates independently of Zagar as a nonprofit art environment. It showcases the work of talented and unique artists from around the world. You can see the work in their indoor and outdoor galleries when you visit.

In 2008, Philadelphia's Magic Gardens opened to the public. Visitors can tour, do art activities, play scavenger hunts, as well as participate in workshops, attend exhibitions and concerts.

Elfreth's Alley

Designated a National Historic Landmark, Elfreth's Alley is a famous area in Philadelphia, that consists of a cobblestone alley lined with 32 historic houses.

In the 18th Century Colonial Philadelphia, Elfreth's Alley was home to artisans and tradesmen. Today, two houses built in 1755 function as a museum and gift shop. Guided tours are also available.

Elfreth's Alley doubled as home and business for people of the 18th century. Grocers, carpenters, tailors, and shoemakers lived upstairs and worked out of the first floor of their houses. This changed later on in the 19th century with the advent of the Industrial Revolution. At that time work shifted mainly to factories.

As you walk through Elfreth's Alley, you can time travel to the early American street architecture. The alley charms with its arched windows, relief details, flower boxes, Flemish brickwork, shutters and ironwork.

Love Park

Officially known as John F. Kennedy plaza, the Love Park is most famous for its reproduction of Robert Indiana's 1964 design LOVE sculpture. It was installed in 1976.

Many tourists and locals flock to the iconic sculpture and love to take photos of themselves next to it.

Love park is located just Northwest of the beautiful City Hall. You can also see Benjamin Franklin Parkway, the Philadelphia Museum of Art and the fountain in the background.

Get these books and more in our "Travel and Cities" series:

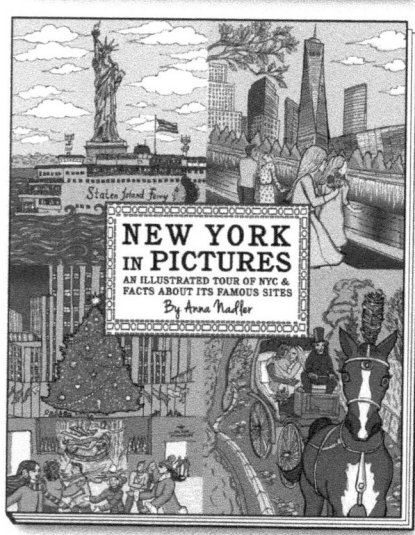

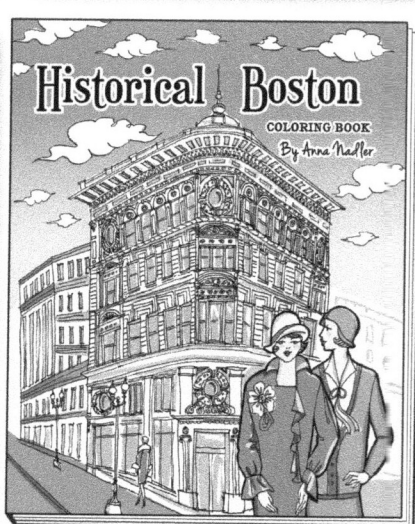

About the Artist

Anna Nadler is an illustrator, graphic designer and author, who lives and works in Staten Island, NY. She loves drawing people, fashion, animals and architecture - trying to capture the unique feeling of every subject she illustrates.

She is always working on new children's books, activity books, coloring books and more.

You can find Anna's books on Amazon and other book retailers.

See more of Anna's illustrations, books, paintings, logo designs, and products on her website - AnnaNadlerArt.com.

Thank you for getting this book!

If you enjoyed it, please leave a review!

The written information included in this book is a combination of various historical facts found in the public domain, respective official websites of the locations included in the book, as well as other widely available online sources. In addition, the author has included her own experiences, after having visited these sites numerous times throughout the years. These are brief summaries designed to introduce you to the locations and are not meant to formally educate you.

Edited by Samuel Anson.

www.ingramcontent.com/pod-product-compliance
Lightning Source LLC
Chambersburg PA
CBHW041525120626

46551CB00018B/2576